ONE DEMON SPIRIT

that controls, dominates, possesses, oppresses, vexes, and torments, 8 out of every 10 people in the world today, including born-again Christians:

FEAR!

By Morris Cerullo

D1502447

Morr   ,Inc.

i

MORRIS CERULLO WORLD EVANGELISM

P.O. Box 85277 • San Diego, CA 92186
(858) 277-2200

E-mail: morriscerullo@mcwe.com
Website: www.mcwe.com

MORRIS CERULLO WORLD EVANGELISM OF CANADA

P.O. Box 3600 • Concord, Ontario L4K-1B6
(905) 669-1788

MORRIS CERULLO WORLD EVANGELISM OF GREAT BRITAIN

P.O. Box 277 • Hemel Hempstead, HERTS HP2-7DH
44 (0)1 442 232432

ONE DEMON SPIRIT

TABLE OF CONTENTS

INTRODUCTION......................i
Could a demon be controlling your life?

ONE...1
Was demon power real in Jesus' day?

TWO...15
Ministers are in torment.

THREE.......................................23
Can a Christian be demon possessed?

FOUR..31
The invisible war for your mind.

FIVE..41
The secret of spiritual strength.

SIX..49
The love that casts out all fear.

SEVEN......................................53
Winning the war, versus winning the battle.

INTRODUCTION

Could a demon be controlling your life?

Demon power is real.

Do you believe it?

I know you say that you do, but do you really believe that Satan's demons could be controlling your life right now?

I'm beginning to discover that even very dedicated Christians don't really understand what is happening to them in the spirit world.

The other day I was deeply concerned when one of my most fervent Partners said to an associate of mine, "There's something about spiritual warfare that I just don't understand."

"What's that?"

"Well, Brother Cerullo says that, 'There is no total victory in spiritual war until we (as Christians) conquer our enemy who has already been defeated.'

"Now, I know that Satan is our enemy, and that demons do exist; but if Jesus already defeated them at Calvary 2,000 years ago, why do we have to conquer them all over again? How could Satan have any real power over Christians if Jesus has already won?"

Unfortunately this thinking is very common.

On one hand, Christians are living lives of torment, walking in bondage and defeat with no real spiritual power.

On the other hand, they know God's Word and have been trained in spiritual warfare, but have little idea of the power and the seriousness of the war they are in.

The bottom line of all their thinking is, "Satan has already been stripped of his power. I'm safe because I'm in Jesus' hands."

Beloved, if this is what you have been telling yourself, you, too, have been blinded by one of the enemy's most brutal deceptions.

Somehow, he has convinced you that all the problems, illnesses, defeats, depressions, and anxieties in your life have nothing to do with demon powers; they are all caused by circumstances, your in-laws, the wrong vitamins, a bad childhood, or anything else you can think of!

But the fact is that demon oppression is very real in the Church today.

There is one demon spirit that controls, dominates, possesses, oppresses, vexes and torments eight out of ten people in the world today...including born-again Christians!

Right now there is an 80 percent chance that this demon spirit is secretly pulling you away from God, destroying your witness for Christ, and choking your growth in the Holy Spirit ...and you don't even know it.

Can you believe it?

I intend to prove it to you.

Let us now turn to the Word of God, for God's infallible Word is the same yesterday, today, and forever.

Chapter 1

WAS DEMON POWER REAL IN JESUS' DAY?

The Bible says that one day a man came to Jesus and pleaded,

> *"Sir, have mercy on my son, for he is mentally deranged and in great trouble, for he often falls into the fire or into the water;"*

MATTHEW 17:15, TLB

What was the boy's problem? Was it psychological, or hereditary? The Bible goes on to plainly state that he was vexed with a demon. For as soon as *"Jesus rebuked the demon in the boy...it left him, and from that moment the boy was well"* (verse 18).

Then, in the Book of Luke we learn of a man from Gadara who was more than insane. When he came to meet Jesus, he was homeless, naked, and lived in a cemetery among the tombs.

The demons took control of the man so often that even when he was shackled with chains he simply broke them apart and rushed into the desert completely under the demons' power.

When attacks and fits of demon activity would come upon him, he would throw himself against rocks until his body was cut open and bleeding. When Jesus asked this demon his

1

name he replied, *"Legion,"* because there were so many! (Luke 8:27-31).

Many people in this "modern, sophisticated" 21st Century would say, "The poor man probably had a severe hormone imbalance." Or, "I know that kind of behavior is the result of a traumatic childhood." Or, "I guess he was just born a "bad seed."

But that's not what the Bible says. The Bible says it was the work of demon spirits, pure and simple.

The Word of God proves that this man was not just a "bad seed" with a chemical problem because when he was delivered of all those foul spirits he immediately became an outstanding evangelist (Luke 8:33-39).

We could go on and on, proving in case after case that demon power was real in Jesus' day. Not only was it real, but it severely tormented, oppressed, possessed, vexed and controlled many people of biblical times.

Demons caused deafness, blindness, and countless other ailments that destroyed the minds and bodies, not only of the "heathen," but of God's very own people.

IS DEMON POWER REAL TODAY?

Now, I want you to take a little imaginary trip with me.

Come into a mental institution for the insane such as is found in many of your cities. I want you to take a good look around as we walk inside.

There's a woman who comes to greet us at the door. She's wearing a white uniform, and has long keys dangling from her side. Let us have no delusions about what those keys unlock.

They unlock cold, clammy, gray steel doors that house human beings just like you and I: people who are caged behind bars.

You look inside one of those cages and what do you see?

You see a person just like you crouched against solid cement walls. On these walls you can see indentations as deep as your fingers that have been made by bleeding, human hands.

Next we walk to the place where they keep the "hard cases." There's one skinny little man there, and it is taking five men to get that one human being into a straitjacket.

Sound familiar?

Like someone you just met in the country of Gadara in the Bible?

Tell me, where do you think he gets his superhuman strength?

As we watch, we see that it takes one 250-pound male nurse to hold down each one of his arms, and two more to hold down his body and his legs. Meanwhile, another man tries to squeeze him into that straitjacket; the only thing they have to control him.

Why? Because that man is possessed with superhuman power.

That same superhuman demon power that was so real two thousand years ago is just as real today.

If you don't believe me, pick up your morning newspaper and ask yourself, "What makes a man 19 years of age strangle a beautiful young lady he has never seen before?"

"What makes a young mother take her seven-day old infant, stuff her into a trash can, close the lid, and leave her there to die?"

The Bible tells us exactly what makes her do it: It is the same demon power that tried to murder that "mentally deranged" boy by throwing him into the fire!

Again, we could go on and on with modern day examples of demon power and not even uncover the tip of the iceberg.

In Jesus' day, the reality of demon power was never questioned. People knew it existed, pure and simple. The only thing that amazed them was that there was finally Someone around Who had the power over the devil to do something about it.

And do something He did. Jesus dealt with all of these gruesome situations in short order. How? With power and authority He commanded each one of those foul spirits to leave, and they did!

The public was astounded.

> ..."*What new doctrine is this? For with authority He commands even the unclean spirits, and they obey Him.*"
>
> MARK 1:27, NKJ

By now you may be saying, "All right, Brother Cerullo, I've read my newspaper. I'll admit that Satan has great power in the world today.

"But all those things I read about are with unsaved people. The devil can't get away with those atrocities in born-again Christians. We're protected by the blood of the Lamb. Jesus died to save us from all that."

You're absolutely right. Jesus did die to save us from "all that." However, "all that" is still going on. Why?

Let me ask you a question: do we have people in the Church today who are deaf? People who can't speak? People who have mental problems? People who are constantly ill?

Jesus has plainly shown us that many of these afflictions are a direct result of demon oppression. (See Matthew 12:28, 43;

Mark 1:23, 26; 7:25; 9:17-26; Luke 4:33; 8:29; 9:42 and 13:11).

In addition, we see the utter devastation caused by broken homes, child abuse, and divorce which is rampant in the Church today.

These are the very things that God sent His Son to this earth to destroy.

> *"...for this purpose the Son of God was manifested, that He might destroy the works of the devil."*
>
> I JOHN 3:8, NKJ

He then put all the keys to spiritual power in our hands to finish the job. He has given us power over all the power of the enemy (Luke 10:19).

Then why haven't we done something about all those tormented, demon oppressed brothers and sisters sitting right next to us in the pews as we listen to sermons about "love" week after week?

My Bible says that just as Jesus is in heaven (the everlasting Conqueror), so are we to be right now in this world (I John 4:17).

Who is Jesus?

He is the Victor. He is a Man of war against all the destructive forces of the devil.

What are we?

We are so bound and oppressed that I am concerned many Christians are literally on their way to being spit out of His mouth! (See Revelation 3:16).

URGENT ALARM!

Today the Lord is urgently sounding the alarm, trying to make us see that many people in the Church who have assumed they will be part of the marriage feast, could instead be cast out of His kingdom if they insist on living with the oppressive forces that are binding them and destroying Christ's Church. These oppressive forces are making you, as a Christian, both helpless and useless.

I want to read to you one of the most chilling stories in the Word of God...a story that haunts me day and night— a story that keeps me awake grieving for God's blinded, oppressed, dominated and controlled people.

I know of nothing that shows how a Christian can be rendered helpless, uselessly bound by Satan, more than the story Jesus Himself tells in Matthew 25:14-30. Open your Bible with me now as the Lord reveals to us the horrifying truth of how Satan oppresses God's people in the Church.

The story begins as Matthew tells of how the Master, Jesus, went away on a far journey. But before He left He invested in His servants, entrusting them with all He had.

Read this dramatic passage of Scripture with me now:

"For the kingdom of heaven is as a man travelling into a far country, who called his own servants, and delivered unto them his goods.

And unto one he gave five talents, to another two, and to another one; to every man according to his several ability; and straightway took his journey.

Then he that had received the five talents went and traded with the same, and made them other five talents.

And likewise he that had received two, he also gained other two.

But he that had received one went and digged in the earth, and hid his lord's money.

After a long time the lord of those servants cometh,

and reckoneth with them.

And so he that had received five talents came and brought other five talents, saying, Lord, thou deliveredst unto me five talents: behold, I have gained beside them five talents more.

His lord said unto him, Well done, thou good and faithful servant: thou hast been faithful over a few things, I will make thee ruler over many things: enter thou into the joy of thy lord.

He also that had received two talents came and said, Lord, thou deliveredst unto me two talents: behold, I have gained two other talents beside them.

His lord said unto him, Well done good and faithful servant; thou hast been faithful over a few things, I will make thee ruler over many things: enter thou into the joy of thy Lord.

Then he which had received the one talent came and said, Lord, I knew thee that thou art a hard man, reaping where thou hast not sown, and gathering where thou hast not strawed:

And I was afraid, and went and hid thy talent in the earth: lo, there thou hast that is thine.

His lord answered and said unto him, Thou wicked and slothful servant, thou knewest that I reap where I sowed not, and gather where I have not strawed:

Thou oughtest therefore to have put my money to the exchangers, and then at my coming should have received mine own with usury.

Take therefore the talent from him, and give it unto him which hath ten talents.

For unto every one that hath shall be given, and he shall have abundance: but from him that hath not shall be taken away even that which he hath.

*And cast ye the unprofitable servant into outer darkness:
there shall be weeping and gnashing of teeth."*
MATTHEW 25:14-30

Now, why did the Master react like this? Was it because the servant went out and lived with prostitutes? Was it because he lived a riotous life of drinking and gambling? Was he a liar or a thief?

No. This man had already been chosen to be a servant of Christ. He was already called to be a member of the Kingdom of God, just like you and I.

But he was cast out of the Kingdom because he allowed his life in Christ to be controlled and dominated by one particular demon agent in Satan's army.

Yes, this man was literally vexed and tormented to such a degree that he needed deliverance. He was like so many people in the world today (even born-again Christians), who are useless to God and feel helpless to do anything about it.

Remember that this parable was Jesus' way of giving us a deep spiritual truth with which to warn us of a major spiritual pitfall.

Earlier in the book of Matthew, Jesus warns us that not everyone who cries, *"Lord, Lord,"* is going to live with Him in heaven, but only he who does the will of the Father (Matthew 7:21).

Yet, on that final day this servant said (in essence) to the Master, "I was afraid. I went out and hid your talent in the ground. I hid the resources you gave me to save souls because I was ruled by fear. I could not do Your will because fear ruled my mind, my spirit, my emotions, and my actions. I was afraid."

Like you and me, this servant had everything he needed to do the will of God. He was called for the Kingdom and was fully equipped for what he had to do. He had been given the same ability, power, and relationship with God as the servants who were given two talents and five talents.

But on that final day, he had nothing with which to meet the Master but a feeble excuse for not making his life count for God.

I do not know of another power that can render you as helpless and useless; that can tie your hands, bind your mind, control, vex and torment your soul like the spirit of fear!

Fear is a spirit!

The Apostle Paul warned Timothy,

"For God has not given us a spirit of fear, but of power and of love and of a sound mind."

II TIMOTHY: 1:7, NKJ

The Word also tells us that *"Fear hath torment"* (I John 4:18). Therefore, since fear is a tormenting spirit, we know that it does not come from God.

If it does not come from God, there is only one other source fear can come from, and that is from Satan!

It is the devil's goal to keep you oppressed by fear; to prevent you from doing the will of God and to keep you from being used by God in the gifts of the Spirit.

Fear is one way Satan keeps us in bondage to self. When God gives you a gift of His Spirit to give to others, Satan uses fear to make you think, "This might not be God. It's probably just me, and I'll make a fool of myself. I'd better hold back."

Fear is also the devil's tool to keep us in bondage to the opinions of man...we are afraid of what people will think or say about us. We become afraid that we might not be accepted in our denominations if we go all the way for God.

I know of nothing that binds, vexes, torments, and keeps

us from doing God's will any more than fear.

When we attend a spiritual meeting, God moves upon our hearts to give in order to reach the lost.

But as soon as we get home Satan attacks: "You can't give that amount. It's too much. You were just being emotional. What will happen if you get cancer or lose your job? You have so little money in the bank."

Fear strikes and God is robbed. Satan has won the victory. The door is now open for the enemy to come in and hinder the glorious promises of God.

The unholy spirit of fear takes control. The Kingdom suffers.

Remember that judgment begins in the house of God (I Peter 4:17). If you go down to defeat to the spirit of fear, what will you say when you stand before God?

Friend, if you have ever made a pledge to God and not fulfilled that vow, I urge you to do so before you go one step further. I don't want you to stand before the Master and hear what the unprofitable servant heard. Jesus told him, "Depart from me" and he was cast into outer darkness.

We are to be ruled by love for our Lord, never by fear! The book of Ecclesiastes tells us:

> *"When you vow a vow or make a pledge to God, do not put off paying it; for God has no pleasure in fools (those who witlessly mock Him). Pay what you vow. "It is better that you should not vow than that you should vow and not pay."* (cf. Psalms 50:14; 66:13,14; 76:11).

ECCLESIASTES 5:4,5

Let us each determine today to overcome all fear so that we might glorify God by triumphantly saying to Him, *"Praise is awaiting You, O God, in Zion; And to You the vow shall be performed"* (Psalm 65:1, NKJ).

Beloved, it's harvest time! This is not a fire drill...it's the real thing. Jesus is coming! Let us all get our houses in order quickly and, using all the resources at our disposal, move on to total victory in Him.

FEAR RULES GOD'S SERVANTS TODAY

This unprofitable servant was afraid to use the resources God had given him to use; and he refused to use the tools God had given him to overcome his fear.

However, as sad as this story sounds, it is nothing compared to what is going on with God's servants today.

If you don't believe me, just read several of the hundreds of letters I receive from Christians each week, Christians whose lives are fruitless and in complete bondage to the spirit of fear.

One friend writes,

> "Brother Morris, I have agoraphobia (an abnormal fear of public places). I've been saved over three years, but God hasn't healed me yet. Please pray that the Lord Jesus will heal me of this torment so that I can go out and speak of Him and get a job."

Now listen to the way Satan has another dear Christian so paralyzed by fear that she is totally useless in fulfilling God's will for her life. She pleads:

> "Dear Brother Cerullo and Theresa, please help me. I can't cope with this three year old problem that seems to be getting worse. I really need help.
>
> "Why is it that I have the most difficult time maintaining eye contact with anyone? On account of it, I fear people. I find it so difficult to fellowship with anyone. Even my relationship with my husband is

shaky, and I have problems trying to communicate with my child.

"I don't have any friends. There are people who want my friendship, but it seems that I can't let them. I retreat from them with a sort of weird look in my eyes, and with a fearful and timid attitude.

"It's such a helpless feeling that overwhelms me. I almost have to force myself to go anywhere.

"I asked God not long ago to give me a burden for people so that I could reach out to them and give myself to them.

"Well, praise God, the burden is there, but the problem is that whenever there's a need for me to reach out I panic. I get frightened and find it difficult to even face them.

"What is this? I know that God did not create me this way. There are people in need everywhere, and here I am...just wasting my life."

I hope your heart is breaking as you see the desperation in this life. These same fears may be yours.

Yet God's Word commands that we must (and can) rise up and overcome all our fears. All those who do not overcome will be cast into the lake of fire, right along with all the other "unprofitable" agents of Satan.

"But the fearful, and unbelieving, and the abominable, and murderers, and whoremongers, and sorcerers, and idolaters, and all liars, shall have their part in the lake which burneth with fire and brimstone: which is the second death."

REVELATION 21:8

I know this is not a passage that many of you have underlined in your Bibles. Yet it is just as true as all the

12

promises for prosperity, health, and happiness that we're so fond of.

Believe me, if God's Word says something, we have two choices: We can either take it very seriously, or fall into deceit.

Which do you choose?

When you stand before your Lord on that final day, are you going to face Him with the many "treasures" of lost souls that you've won and nurtured...or a lot of feeble excuses of why you were afraid to step out?

> ..."For everyone to whom much is given, from him
> much will be required; and to whom much has been
> committed, of him they will ask the more."
>
> LUKE 12:48, NKJ

Are you going to say, "Yes, Lord. I obeyed your every command. I took every tool you gave me, overcame my fears, and was victorious for you."

Or, are you going to say, "Well, I know Your Word said, 'Fear not,' but I didn't think that applied to me. You see, I had a burden to pray for the sick, but I was afraid to learn to drive, so I never got far from my house."

Or, "I was the shy type, so I never got into witnessing. I did play the piano in Sunday school, though. Wasn't that enough?"

Or, "I was afraid that if I tithed I wouldn't have enough for myself. I was afraid to trust You to provide for me."

So what was the unprofitable servant's excuse for being afraid? Fear of poverty!

He told the Lord,

> "Sir, I knew you were a hard man, and **I was afraid
> you would rob me of what I earned**, so I hid your
> money in the earth."
>
> MATTHEW 25:25, TLB

What about you? Are you in bondage to fear of giving because you're afraid that the Lord might ask you for more, or that the "well will run dry?"

Many of you are in such bondage to fear that you are afraid to receive healing from God.

So many are like the little woman who came to me at a meeting in West Virginia, hobbling on two great big canes.

I said to this lady, "In the Name of Jesus, drop those canes."

She said, "I can't do that."

"Why not?[a]

"Because I'm afraid I will fall."

At that point I put my hand on her and cast out the spirit of fear, in the Name of Jesus. Then I grabbed those two canes and pulled them out from under her while her eyes were closed.

Then I gave her a little push and said, "Now, get going."

She had only two alternatives: One was to fall and the other was to walk. She decided she would walk and was totally healed, but there are many who decide they will not.

I tell you, the Church today is being ruled by a spirit of fear. Because of this, hundreds of thousands of "born-again" Christians who think they're in good shape with the Lord, are sinking fast into "unprofitable servanthood." This includes pastors, ministers, and evangelists. Yes, the spirit of fear is not only ruling the pews, it's in the pulpit too.

Chapter 2

MINISTERS ARE IN TORMENT

Unfortunately, we live in an age and in a society where the image we have of our local minister (or evangelist, or teacher) is of someone high on a pedestal, three miles removed from the anguish of tormenting fears of Satan.

The minister then feels a tremendous inner burden to live up to his stainless steel image. Tremendous energy drains out of his innermost being as he struggles day after day to "keep the mask on." Publicly, he usually succeeds.

But the turmoil raging inside his soul is another matter. There he carries on more wars with fear and anxiety than most of us could ever deal with.

One typical example is a pastor who recently wrote to me in desperation. He said:

"Brother Cerullo, we are a pastor family in a 'holiness' denomination, and we are filled with the Spirit. But we are battling with the problem of being very double minded. We are being tortured by Satan with fears, doubts, and fears of rejection—unable to stand firm.

"When God leads us to pray for the sick or to work miracles, we are beginning to take courage to do it. In many cases, while we are beginning to pray or move on it, fear hits us and we are not able to complete the work."

This man is not alone.

There is another fine pastor in Massachusetts whom I love dearly, but who is another example of how fear is robbing preachers (and their entire congregations) of the glory and power of God.

One day this man told me that he would be one of my main supporters if I held a meeting in his city. So I went to that city, and God gave us a great meeting.

However, as I looked around for this pastor, I could not find him. God was shaking the place with His Presence, but this man (who had the largest Full Gospel church in the area) never showed up.

After I had been there several weeks I got a phone call from him. He said, "Brother Cerullo, I would have been so happy to sponsor your revival."

I said, "Then why weren't you out?"

He answered, "Please pray for me. I would have been there if I could, but I couldn't. I'm afraid."

"Afraid of what?"

"I'm afraid of my deacon board."

He went on to tell me that just before I came to town they had started a radio broadcast. According to him, "We're beginning to get some nice people in the church. The deacons were afraid that if the folks knew we were connected with a meeting like yours, we might lose them. We carry on such a big program that we can't afford to have anything happen."

I said, "Brother, how many people did you get out for your Sunday night service?"

He murmured, "About 40 or 50."

Where was the rest of the town? They were at our meeting.

All those people that his deacons were so worried about scaring away were at our place...some of them until 2 o'clock in the morning getting the Baptism of the Holy Ghost.

Oh, how fear of man is keeping hundreds of thousands of people and their pastors not only away from the blessings of God, but away from obeying Jesus and moving out in the power of God!

Pastors are afraid of their congregations; congregations are afraid of their pastors; pastors are afraid of each other...afraid that the church down the street might get a few more tithe paying sheep.

I can just hear the agonizing cry of our Lord as He warns and pleads with us:

> *"My friends, do not be afraid of those who kill the body, and after that have no more that they can do. But I will show you whom you should fear: Fear Him who, after He has killed, has power to cast into hell; yes, I say to you, fear Him!"*

LUKE 12:4-6, NKJ

A few years ago another pastor confided, "I really don't want to teach spiritual warfare. Talking about Satan might scare people."

But, praise God, this man got the victory over the fears in his own life and today is raising up one of the most powerful youth armies for God in the country! His congregation has more than doubled.

Right now, God is looking for thousands of pastors, ministers, and evangelists like this man.

Before Christ returns, He is going to purge His body of all the dead works we've been locked into out of fear; all the cold, joyless formalism which holds congregations in bondage because their pastors are afraid of the Spirit of God.

How my heart grieves to see so many of you, who long to sing, to testify, and to move out in the gifts of the Holy Spirit, hold back because you're afraid you will say the wrong thing. You hold words of life "in your hands," and are afraid to deliver them!

There are whole congregations who are terrified to lift up their hands to the Lord, or to issue a prayer request at a small gathering. Of course, giving a prophecy or a message in tongues is out of the question!

So many people long to see the gifts of the Holy Spirit in operation (the gifts that God gave us to build and equip His Church), but the pastors are so afraid of their people "getting in the flesh" that they never get in the Spirit.

One man started to get the Baptism of the Holy Ghost in my meeting. He began to speak in other tongues; then all of a sudden he stopped.

I asked him, "Why did you stop after you started to speak?"

He answered, "When I started speaking it sounded like I myself was speaking. I got to thinking that it was me and not God, and I became afraid."

You do not have to be afraid. God, your Father, will not give you something that isn't of Him (Luke 11:11,13).

Do not be afraid to "let go."

The Word of God commands us,

> *"Never lag in zeal and in earnest endeavor; be aglow and burning with the Spirit, serving the Lord."*
>
> ROMANS 12:11, AMP

God literally dwells in the praises of His people (Psalm 22:3). You need never be afraid to use all the "talents" He Himself has put within you to enable you to worship Him in spirit and in truth.

You do not have to fear anybody else's opinion when He gives you a word which will heal or encourage one of His suffering lambs. You need only to stand up and give it!

If you insist on living in fear of "being emotional" or of "being in the flesh" you will never know what it is like to be used of God in the Spirit.

But you say, "Wait a minute, Brother Cerullo, I'm not one of those people who is bound by fear. I'm fine."

You are? Then let me ask you, how many souls have you won to Christ during the past 12 months?

How about in the last six months? Three months?

How many unpaid vows do you have?

How often have you used your "talents" to proclaim God's Word to the lost To heal the sick? To bind up someone who is brokenhearted, or to set one of Satan's captives free?

What kind of excuse are you going to present to the Master?

Jesus has ordained that,

> *"You shall receive power when the Holy Spirit has come upon you; and you shall be witnesses to Me in Jerusalem, and in all Judea and Samaria, and to the end of the earth."*
>
> ACTS 1:8, NKJ

Yet, Satan is keeping many of you so bound by fear that you can't even witness to your neighbor or fellow worker at your job.

The strongest satanic deception in the Church today is that Satan's demons operate only outside the body; that when it comes to Christians, these demons have no real power.

Meanwhile, the demon spirit of fear is keeping a majority of God's people tied up in fruitless bondage, deceived into thinking that it's all right to sit back and wait for heaven—when in reality they are headed for "outer darkness."

All this directly relates to Satan's second most destructive deception.

THE SECOND MOST DESTRUCTIVE DECEPTION

There are literally thousands of different fears that bind the Church today. Every day we face fear of cats, trees, cars, airplanes; fear of being alone, of being rejected, of being around people; fear of intimacy, of relationships, of responsibility, of commitment; fear of poverty, success, losing what you have, the opinions of others, and impending sicknesses.

But the one deception that Satan has succeeded in pulling off, in the minds of all those who fear, is that failure to overcome your little fear is no big deal because it affects you and you alone.

Let me tell you something. No fear that you hang onto or fail to get victory over ever affects only you alone!

We are all one in the Spirit, and any fear which hinders you, ultimately has a devastating effect on the whole Body of Christ in the spirit world.

This is why God has always refused to allow the fearful to remain in His Army! In essence He told them, "Go home. We don't want you. We don't need you. When we go to war you'll only contaminate the others." (Read Deuteronomy 20:8 and Judges 7:3)

In God's Army today it doesn't matter what your fear is. The truth is that all fear emanates from a demon spirit of fear who has gained a foothold in your mind, and is an archenemy of God.

If this spirit of fear is allowed to retain its foothold, sooner or later it will rise up to hinder, block, and prevent Christ's life from flowing through you when you need it the most.

Friend, are you ready to do something about it?

In many ways God's Army today is like the children of Israel were when they came out of Egypt. After they were delivered, what was the first thing they were faced with?

The Red Sea!

What was their reaction to it?

They were paralyzed with fear!

Fear literally overtook their minds as they turned against Moses, complaining,

> *"Have you brought us out here to die in the desert because there were not enough graves for us in Egypt?"*
>
> EXODUS 14:11, TLB

At first Moses desperately tried to encourage them by telling them to hang in there. "Just stand still," he said. "The Lord will fight for you."

But at that point the Lord Himself broke in with a direct command:

> *"Quit praying and get the people moving! Forward, march!"*
>
> EXODUS 14:15, TLB

These are the same orders our Commander is giving us now.

He is telling us that it's time to quit whining about our fears and time to get moving in our offensive warfare against the devil.

Therefore, as of today you and I are going to go after every demon power of fear that is binding your life and destroying your witness for Christ!

You say, "Brother Cerullo, you sound angry."

I am angry...not at you, but at Satan for robbing you of Christ's riches in this life, and of your reward in His Kingdom to come.

We are going to stop this now! We are going to rip the mask right off the devil (and his tactics), openly and without fear.

I have exposed his strategies and am providing you with a foundation for conquering him in every aspect of your life.

You are not going to hide. You are not going to remain on the defensive. You are not fighting a war of preservation.

God's Word has already told us why He sent His Son to deliver us. It was:

> *"To grant us that we, being delivered from the*
> *hand of our enemies, might serve Him without fear,*
> *in holiness and righteousness before Him all the*
> *days, of our life."*
>
> LUKE 1:74-75, NKJ

Bless God, you have heard His battle cry against fear in your heart.

You are now going to come down out of your high tower of head knowledge and move out onto the battlefield.

All the joy, courage, confidence, peace, vitality and zeal that Satan has stolen from you through fear will be restored to you in the mighty Name of Jesus.

> *"For God has not given us a spirit of fear, but of*
> *power and of love and of a sound mind"*
>
> II TIMOTHY 1:7, NKJ

Get ready. You are about to begin a victorious life!

Chapter 3

CAN A CHRISTIAN BE DEMON POSSESSED?

Before we explore the keys to overcoming fear, I'd like to answer one question with which I'm sure many of you are eager to challenge me. That is, "Brother Cerullo, are you telling me that a born-again Christian can be demon possessed?"

The answer is no; at least not in the way that we usually think of "possession." Let me explain.

First of all, there is no distinction in the Bible between oppression, possession, vexation, or anything else that demons can do to you.

The word used in the New Testament for anyone suffering from demonic pressure was "daimonizomai. " The modern interpretation of this word would be "demonized."

To further understand what it means to be demonized, you might ask: "What kind of spirit is in control of (or ruling) my life any time I react in great fear?"

For instance, if you suddenly turn pale, go into a cold sweat, tremble and start screaming when you become frightened, what kind of spirit would you say is in control of your mind at that moment? The Spirit of God, or the spirit of fear?

Or, if you become violently ill when you even think about getting on an airplane, which spirit is ruling your mind at that time?

I'll tell you, it sure isn't the Spirit of God.

Then where is God when all this is happening? You KNOW that you've accepted Jesus as your personal Savior; you know that you have received His Holy Spirit. If this is so, then where is He when these vicious fears strike?

Beloved, your Lord has promised that He will never leave you or forsake you (Hebrews 13:5). Therefore, He is right there all the time, standing by in your new inner self.

You say, "Why is He `standing by,' Brother Cerullo? Why doesn't He do something?"

Believe me, He wants to, if you will only learn how to let Him.

He is waiting for you to call on Him in those moments of hidden terror: He is waiting for you to learn to recognize His Presence within you, and to tap into His power so that He might rise up from within you and defeat the enemy.

CHRIST'S LIFE WITHIN YOU
CAN NEVER BE 'POSSESSED'

You see, that perfect seed of Christ's life which was planted within you when you were born again can never be possessed, oppressed, or in any way infiltrated by the enemy.

It is impregnable: incapable of being assaulted or penetrated by any outside, evil force.

However, that precious seed of Christ's life in your inner man is like a tiny embryo encased by the outer "shell" of your old nature.

During your years of spiritual growth, this outer shell will begin to crack, crumble, and eventually fall away as the "new person" within you starts to grow and emerge.

This process is much like a baby chick coming out of its shell. Step by step the chick becomes stronger and stronger as it pecks its way out, until one day it totally breaks through to the outside world.

Through all this, the chick is being mightily strengthened from within by having to break through its shell. By the time the chick does break through its shell, it is strong enough to cope with its new world.

Likewise, you too are emerging as a totally new person in Christ. The Word of God assures you:

"if anyone is in Christ, he is a new creation; old things have passed away; behold, all things have become new."

II CORINTHIANS 5:17, NKJ

You say, "But, Brother Cerullo, this verse says that all old things (like my old fears) have passed away. Then why do I still have them?"

One biblical truth you will come to discover is that no promises in the Bible are simply dumped into our laps.

From cover to cover, the Word of God is about pressing through to (and for) God.

It is a Book about laboring and overcoming through Christ.

The children of Israel found this out the hard way. From the days of Abraham, God had allotted the Promised Land to them.

Yet isn't it strange that they couldn't just walk into it after years in the wilderness, kick up their feet and say, ."Oh, Hallelujah! God gave us this land and it's ours. We'll just settle down."

Why couldn't they do this? Because the Promised Land was filled with enemies, and brother, they had to fight a battle to take every inch of the promise.

It's the same with our soul. Jesus has already paid the price to redeem it. But by the time you were born again, that mind of yours was infested with every kind of fear, negative thought pattern, rotten attitude, and worldly reasoning that the devil could pack into it.

So just as Canaan wasn't automatically purged of the

resident enemies when the Israelites walked in, all your fears didn't get automatically washed from your mind the day you said, "I love You, Jesus."

What did happen when you were born again was that you were cleansed from the guilt of all your sins and fears. You were not automatically freed from the power of sin or the power of fear.

That is why there is a spiritual war raging in your life right now; a war in which you:

> *"For we do not wrestle against flesh and blood, but against principalities, against powers, against the rulers of the darkness of this age, against spiritual hosts of wickedness in the heavenly places."*
>
> EPHESIANS 6.12, NKJ

Jesus Christ is coming back for a bride "without spot or wrinkle" (Ephesians 5:27). When you came to Him you were not without spot or wrinkle. The "land" of your mind and soul were a mess.

This is the reason you must fight to reclaim the territory of your mind by overcoming a foe who has already been defeated.

Yes, Satan was defeated by Jesus. But through the power of Christ in us, we, too, must conquer him.

Through our Lord Jesus Christ, God has given to you all the authority, all the ability, and all the power to become perfect in Him.

He has given you all you need to lay hold of Christ's victory and be more than conquerors (Romans 8:37). You have been fully equipped with everything necessary to grow up into the mature, perfect bride for His Son.

Obviously, Satan does not want you to use what God has given you. He wants to keep you in bondage to him (through fear), so that you never become an acceptable bride. The only way Satan can do this is to find a foothold in your unrenewed mind; to "roar" at you with fearful thoughts, and hope you accept them.

The worst thing you can do when this happens is to run back into your shell, or give in to these fears.

However, God has no intention of letting you give in or go down to defeat. He intends for you to emerge strong and triumphant. God says:

"...and if he draws back and shrinks in fear, My soul has no delight or pleasure in him. But our way is not of those who draw back to eternal misery... but we are of those who believe who cleave to and trust in and rely on God through Jesus Christ, the Messiah and by faith preserve the soul."

HEBREWS 10:38-39, TAB

I will warn you now that Satan will try to latch onto every fear you have ever had in the past, in an effort to press in and strangle that new spiritual life within you. His goal is to see that you never reach spiritual maturity.

Don't be afraid! Think of Satan's demon spirit of fear as a big, black baboon that is trying to hang onto the "cage" of your old, unrenewed self.

There he is, rattling it, shaking it, screeching at you, trying with all his might to get you to shrink back in fear and stifle that tiny light inside.

His aim is to so thoroughly possess your old nature, that the new person within you never has a chance.

You must resist! This is why spiritual growth is not easy.

The Apostle Paul himself said,

"My little children, of whom I travail in birth again until Christ be formed in you."

GALATIANS 4:19

As Paul found out, getting people "saved" was the easy part. Getting them to grow up to be spiritually mature and victorious is a different matter.

It is not automatic.

The Apostle John reinforces this when he tells us, *"...as many as received him, to them gave he power to become the sons of God..."* (John 1:12).

Some don't make it.

Five (50 percent) of the "ten virgins" who went out to meet the bridegroom (Jesus) were shut out of the wedding feast (Matthew 25:1-10).

Can you imagine a 50 per cent fatality rate in the Church today?

I can.

Why?

Because of fear.

So, are you ready to do something about all those treacherous fears that are haunting your life?

If you are, then let's get started.

FEAR IS A 'CREATIVE' FORCE

The first step to overcoming any problem is to understand it.

In our case we must fully understand that the spirit of fear is actually a powerful force for evil which can "create" or call into being the very thing that is feared.

Job experienced this when he said,

"For the thing which I greatly feared is come upon me, and that which I was afraid of is come unto me."
JOB 3:25

This being so, how does evil power work?

Ever since God created the universe, spiritual powers have had dominion over mental powers; and the powers of the mind have had dominion over the physical realm.

Therefore, whatever spirits we choose to accept into our minds will determine what will be manifested in our physical realm.

For example, if you choose to allow the spirit of fear in your life, you will think fearful thoughts, speak fearful words; and what you fear will eventually come to pass.

If you choose to accept God's Spirit of peace, then you will think peaceful thoughts, speak in peace, and create serenity all around you.

Make no mistake, there are only two kinds of spiritual forces in the world: those that are of God (for good), and those that are of Satan (for evil).

You have the Spirit above all spirits (the Spirit of God) dwelling deep in your innermost being. But the crucial question you must still face daily is, "Which spirit, the Spirit of God, or the spirit of fear, will I choose to accept into my mind today? Which kind of thoughts will I accept or reject?"

Be warned that whichever side you permit to control your thoughts, that side will control your entire being.

> *"Do you not know that to whom you present yourselves slaves to obey, you are that one's slaves whom you obey, whether of sin to death, or of obedience to righteousness?"*
>
> ROMANS 6:16 NKJ

FEAR IS A FACT, BUT FEAR IS AN ACT

I have often taught "Faith is a fact, but faith is an act."

What I have meant is that faith, as a creative spiritual force, is not manifested in the physical realm until you choose with your mind and your will to bring it into being by acting on it.

29

Fear works the same way. Satan can roar at you all he wants to, but if you refuse to let his fearful thoughts dwell in your mind and refuse to act on them, there's nothing more he can do. He will flee from your resistance!

However, if you choose to act on the suggestions planted by the spirit of fear (or use the words of your mouth to reinforce them), you have released a powerful evil force to start working.

What's more, acting and reacting to fear soon becomes a dangerous habit which is very hard to break.

This is why in the Garden of Eden, Satan wasted no time in going after Eve's mind. He knew that if she accepted his suggestions in her mind, these thoughts would then feed her will. And once she chose (with her will) to act on them, she was his.

Chapter 4

THE INVISIBLE WAR
FOR YOUR MIND

In the invisible, spiritual war for our minds, we will see how the spirit of fear leads us directly into unbelief; and unbelief prevents the promises of God from being received in your life.

By studying Satan's operations, we can see that all fear is based on his success in planting seeds of deception in our minds, (particularly our imaginations), and getting us to act on them.

In the Church today we hear so much about faith and living the life of faith. But do you know why most people can't exercise true faith? Because they don't have their minds and their imaginations under control.

The Bible says that Faith is the substance of things hoped for, the evidence of things not seen" (Hebrews 11:1). When you hope for something, you know exactly what you are hoping for because you picture it in your mind. What you visualize actually shapes what you will become! (Proverbs 23:7).

Therefore, faith is the manifestation (or the evidence) of whatever mental pictures you build up in your mind.

Yet, many of you are living in such a state of defeat in your minds that you can't imagine that you really are the overcomer that God says you are! You can't imagine that you have total victory over the fears within you. You can't even imagine how you would act if you were fearless.

You do not have the mental picture of yourself that God wants you to have, based on His Word. Instead of seeing yourself as a new person in Christ (fully trusting Him to empower you to overcome), you see only the negative things that dominated your old nature. You are possessed with the past.

In your mind's eye you see a whole life of failures based on fears...fears that keep cropping up in your imagination as you yield to them and feed on them.

I don't believe there's a person reading this book who hasn't been attacked by fear in his imagination.

For example, from earliest childhood we are programmed by the devil to expect (see ourselves in) poor health in our old age. In our imagination we just know that we will end up with arthritis. We expect our joints to tighten up, our minds to get dull, and our hearing to go bad.

People are constantly telling me, "This illness runs in my family. My father had this pain all his life, and now I've got it. I always knew I'd get it."

Where do they get such vain imaginations? Not from the Spirit of God! They are all fueled by fear.

This is why the Spirit of God specifically told Paul that we must rise up and cast down every vain, foul imagination that comes against us (II Corinthians 2:5). Our imagination is the first stronghold that we must bring under control if we are to thoroughly conquer fear.

Did you know that most people who commit adultery picture it first? Sin first comes as a thought in our imaginations.

It is the same with fear. Fear first comes as a thought from the enemy. If we refuse to rebuke it, suddenly we're ruled by it.

To illustrate this, let's look at a typical example of how this is working in the Church.

Imagine that you have joined a new fellowship and are eager to begin its Wednesday night Bible studies. But when that first Wednesday night rolls around, it's cold and rainy outside.

The spirit of fear taunts your mind and says, "You'd better not go out tonight. The weather is miserable and you're going to get sick."

You accept this thought and help it along in your imagination. "That's right," you say to yourself. "I always get sick if I go out when it's like this. If I get a cold this time I know I'll get pneumonia. I'd better play it safe and stay home just this once."

So you act on the enemy's seed of fear and stay home. Granted, you do not get a cold, but something dangerous and deceptive has happened.

You are now convinced that you remained healthy not because God protected you, but because you stayed home out of the rain!

The next Wednesday night is also chilly and rainy, so you stay home again...unfruitful for God because you're locked into fear of getting a cold.

You have begun to form a habit of obeying the fear instead of obeying God.

As the Apostle Peter warns us:

"...for of whom a man is overcome, of the same is he brought into bondage."

II PETER 2:19, NKJ

You have become a slave to fear. Then one day someone tells you that God would be much more pleased if you would act in faith and get out to that Bible study, rain or no rain.

But by now you're even afraid to drive in the rain. Satan

has progressed to the next stage of drawing you into bondage, for by now you just can't believe that God would see you through.

From this, we can see that all fear is the first step to unbelief.

It is shocking to see how this is exactly the same process which Satan successfully pulled off in the minds of the children of Israel...the same tactics which caused them to fail to enter into the Promised Land of God.

Let's see what took place.

In the book of Numbers, we read how, after years of wandering in the desert, the children of Israel were finally at the gates of the Promised Land. All they had to do was believe God's Word, trust Him, and enter in.

However, they decided to send 12 spies into the territory to check things out first. What happened?

Ten out of the 12 spies disobeyed God by taking their eyes off Him and His promises, and putting them on their enemies instead.

Seeing this, Satan immediately went to work on their minds. By the time the ten stood up to give their report to the people, the spirit of fear had total control of their imaginations.

Instead of expressing faith in God, they could only rebel in unbelief and wail:

> "...The land through which we have gone as spies is a
> land that devours its inhabitants, and all the people
> whom we saw in it are men of great stature There we
> saw the giants...and we were like grasshoppers in our
> own sight, and so we were in their sight."
>
> NUMBERS 13:32,33, NKJ

From this, we learn a very important lesson. That is, Satan's end objective is not merely to keep you in bondage to fear, but to lull you into a state of unbelief through that fear. And unbelief always leads to rebellion against God's Word!

Remember, although Satan had successfully instilled fears in the minds of the children of Israel, God did not ban them from the Promised Land because their imaginations had gone wild.

What really hammered the nails into their coffins was the fact that after they had surrendered to fear, *"...they could not enter in because of unbelief"* (Hebrews 3:19).

Right now, I beg you to realize that your "little fears" are far more dangerous in the long run than you may suspect. Ultimately, each one of them will lead to unbelief and a dangerous denial of God and His Word, which is considered (in His eyes) rebellion.

Please, I beg you to face this question today: "Who has control of my thoughts and my imagination Satan or God?"

DON'T LOOK BACK!

Unfortunately, what happened to the children of Israel was no isolated incident. I see Satan's same "fear tactics" take root in the imaginations of countless Christians day after day.

Just last week a beautiful young lady said, "Please pray for my mother. She had cancer a number of years ago and she just knows it's coming back now"

"Has she been to a doctor?"

"No. She's too depressed to go out because she just knows that it's going to get her this time."

How tragic. Here is a talented woman living a life of secret terror, closed up in her house, bound in torment because

Satan has convinced her that all she can do is get ready to die.

Next, he moves in with self condemnation, guilt, and bitterness. Self-hate and resentment follow, all close companions of fear.

You see, the spirit of fear usually does not work alone. Satan's armies are highly organized, and evil spirits cooperate closely with one another to maintain control of the mind.

Thus, a foothold of fear becomes part of a stronghold; a stronghold housing guilt, isolation, unforgiveness, confusion and more fear.

The torment accelerates as the victim cries, "What's wrong with me. Why hasn't God delivered me?"

Well, what *is* wrong?

One friend pinpointed the problem precisely when she said, "I don't know why I'm afraid, but I've ALWAYS been afraid."

That's it exactly. All fears are based on the past.

All fears depend on you looking back to something that happened to you in the past, even if it was only an hour ago.

Jesus said, *"...if therefore thine eye be single, thy whole body shall be full of light"* (Matthew 6.22).

There is no way that any fear can hover in the dark recesses of your mind when your eye is single-mindedly set on your Lord and His Word.

But you're afraid today because you have your eyes glued to the wrong place. You are being ruled by what has been.

Think about it. Pinpoint your own fears. When did you first experience them?

In childhood? After an auto accident? When your parents were divorced? The first time a door was slammed in your face?

Whatever it was, that incident (or incidents) was a "point of entry" for Satan to plant seeds of guilt and fear in your old nature...and you got stuck there.

You began to talk yourself into believing that all the pain and fears of the past were still real. You kept them alive through your "self-talk."

Make no mistake...words are powerful. Even the silent words you "speak" in conversations with yourself have a dramatic effect on your entire being.

Through your "self-talk" you can literally talk yourself into cooperating with the spirit of fear, and remain in bondage to it.

"If I get close to anybody, they'll only use me so I'd better keep my distance," you say. So, you never get close to anyone not even God.

"I'll never get married. I can't stand all the fighting."

"I hate religion. When I was a kid my folks dragged me to church. I'll never go again."

"I'll never be able to give. We've always been poor."

What you are really saying through all this is, "I really don't believe I'm a new creation in Christ Jesus. I'm afraid to let go; I'm afraid to fully surrender myself to the Lord. I'm afraid to trust him to remold my life. I'll just stay the way I am."

Stop telling yourself these things! The Word of God is commanding you:

"Forget the former things; do not dwell on the past. See, I am doing a new thing Now it springs up; do you not perceive it?"

ISAIAH 43:18-19, NIV

PUT OFF THE OLD MAN

When God first informed Jeremiah that he was called to be a prophet, the boy's first reaction was fear.

"Ah, Lord God!" he cried. "I cannot speak: for I am a child."

God immediately admonished him:

"Say not, I am a child: for thou shalt go to all that I shall send thee...Be not afraid of their faces: for I am with thee to deliver thee...therefore gird up thy loins, and arise...be not dismayed at their faces...For, behold, I have made thee this day a defenced city, and an iron pillar, and brasen walls against the whole land...And they shall fight against thee; but they shall not prevail against thee; for I am with thee, saith the LORD, to deliver thee"

JEREMIAH 1:7,8; 17-19

Notice that the first thing God corrected with Jeremiah was his "self-talk," telling him, "say not!" Then he went after the image that Jeremiah had of himself, changing it from the fearful one that Jeremiah had clung to (based on what he was in the past), to the one that God was shaping for him in the present.

God had great things in store for Jeremiah, but Jeremiah had to face his fears and get rid of his past image first ...starting with his thoughts and the way he talked to himself.

Right now the Word of God promises you that, *"whatever you bind on earth will be bound in heaven"* (Matthew 16:19, NKJ). This includes all those poisonous thoughts that fuel the spirit of fear!

As of today, start binding and casting out those demon-inspired thoughts from your mind. Today is a new day. You are a new creation, and God is commanding you:

*"Strip yourselves of your former nature put off
and discard your old unrenewed self...And be
constantly renewed in the spirit of your mind
having a fresh mental and spiritual attitude; And
put on the new nature...created in God's image."*

EPHESIANS 4:22-24, AMP

Believe me, God would not command you to do something if you could not do it.

The Spirit of God is telling you: "Fear not. Cut the shorelines of your past. A new day is breaking forth upon you. Even now, press through into that which you have spoken unto Me...that which is your, heart's desire. Be free from fear. Step out into My love and you will not sink. You will see My power and My faithfulness in cutting loose those things which have held you in bondage to fear. Release yourself into a new dependence upon Me."

You are ready to press on past the past.

From now on you're going to be able to draw a line and separate the thoughts of your "old self" of the past, from the things the Spirit of God is telling your new self.

This does not mean that all the fears associated with your past will never come up before you again. It does mean that when they do, you are not going to wait five seconds before you successfully deal with them.

How? Read on.

You are about to enter a new dimension of spiritual strength...a new strength that you have never experienced before.

You are about to become an overcomer!

Chapter 5

THE SECRET OF SPIRITUAL STRENGTH

At this point, I know that you have a deep desire to be freed from every one of your fears. But by now you are also aware that if you are ever going to gain victory over fear, there's going to be a fight!

Spiritual battles take energy; energy which you don't think you have right now.

I can just hear you moaning, "Brother Cerullo, where am I ever going to get the strength to fight? The devil has me so wrung out, I don't have one ounce of energy left."

I know you don't. So I'm now going to show you the reason why you have not been able to press through to victory in your battles against fear.

It is because it takes spiritual energy to stand and fight. Spiritual battles cannot be fought in natural strength. Inside, your spiritual well has run dry. Therefore, you've fallen into the habit of retreating or compromising in defeat.

This is what is called a defensive position in warfare. A defensive position doesn't take any energy at all.

An offensive position does.

But you have been too bound by fear to get in touch with God's power within you and fight offensively.

So how do you "tap into" His abundant energy?

There is only one secret to real spiritual strength.

THE TRUTH HIMSELF SHALL MAKE YOU FREE

In the Bible, God promises us that *"If you abide in My word, you are My disciples indeed. And you shall know the truth, and the truth shall make you free"*(John 8:31-32).

Notice that in the first half of His instructions, God established a prerequisite for freedom and that prerequisite is, "If you abide in my word."

In other words, if you do your part by living in total obedience to His Word, then you shall know the truth; and within the truth itself is all the strength and power you need to be fully free.

So the first question I want to ask you is: Are you abiding daily in His Word?

Then let me ask you: If it is the truth itself which makes us free, what is the truth?

Somebody said to me, "The truth is the Word of God."

That is correct. But the Word of God is more than just a written Book.

The Word is also the living word, Who is Jesus Christ Himself!

> *"In the beginning was the Word, and the Word was with God and the Word was God"*
>
> JOHN 1:1

The Living Word, Jesus, is Himself the Living Truth. He said, *"I AM the way, the truth and the life"* (John 14:6).

Therefore, it is the combination of your knowledge of the

written Word with your knowledge of the living Word and living Truth (Jesus Christ) dwelling within you, who is the source of all spiritual strength!

For years, many of you have been faithfully building a good spiritual foundation through your knowledge of the written Word.

You know all about God's plan of salvation, His Great Commission, the keys of binding and loosing, the "Four Spiritual Laws," and everything else.

But those of you who have been paralyzed by fear have not built an equally firm foundation of personal knowledge and the personal experience of Him living within you.

Your relationship with Him has been weak; therefore your spiritual strength has also been weak.

Because you have not been in touch daily with the experience of Christ within you, you have not been free.

You may know a lot about Him through His written Word, but if you don't know him personally, your spiritual "house" will eventually crumble. He Himself warns, *"...apart from Me you can do nothing"*(John 15:5, NKJ).

The Pharisees of Jesus' day had to face this very same issue when Jesus told them:

> *"You search and investigate and pore over the Scriptures diligently, because you suppose and trust that you have eternal life through them. And these (very Scriptures) testify about Me! And still you are not willing (but refuse) to come to Me, so that you might have life"*
> JOHN 5:39-40, AMP

Freedom from fear takes spiritual strength...the kind of strength that can only be drawn from getting in touch with

Christ in you, your hope of glory! (Colossians 1:27).

In the most famous chapter on spiritual warfare ever written, the Apostle Paul says:

> *"...be strong in the Lord be empowered through your union with Him; draw your strength from Him that strength which His boundless might provides"*
> EPHESIANS 6:10, AMP

Remember that five of the ten ladies in Matthew 25 did not have the spiritual strength to make it to the wedding feast. Their lamps had run dry. Why? Until they actually stood face to face with the Lord they had assumed they were in good shape. Instead they were cast out. Why didn't they have the strength to make it in the end?

The Lord gave them the answer. He said, *"...I do not know you"* (Matthew 25:12).

Obviously they knew His written Word and they had gone out to meet Him.

But they had not spent their lives getting to know Him.

The most precious "talent" He gives us is our **time,** and they had not invested it wisely!

I beg you to be aware that it is only through a powerful, personal union with Him that you will ever come to know the true source of spiritual strength.

He is about to give you a breakthrough into the true knowledge of Him, which is the basis of that union.

It is a union of strength.

It is the union of His Love.

BREAK THROUGH TO POWER OVER FEAR

Several years ago, God revealed to me that all truth is parallel.

By this, I mean that man lives in two worlds: the natural realm and the spiritual realm. Nothing happens in one world that doesn't have a "parallel" effect in the other.

In our natural world we are seeing astounding things take place daily. Breakthroughs in science and technology that were considered science fiction only 50 years ago, are now becoming commonplace.

What is a breakthrough?

A breakthrough is a sudden burst of advanced knowledge. It is that sudden burst of revelation where, with a surge of insight, you suddenly look up and say, "I've got it!"

But if all truth is parallel, and these things are happening in the natural world, what is going on in the spiritual world, and in the lives of born-again Christians?

I'll tell you. Right now, God is pouring out His Spirit in a new work of grace and total restoration deep in your inner self...He is taking you into a new spiritual dimension of revelation.

"Revelation of what, Brother Cerullo?"

The revelation of His Son in you!

Remember that our definition of "revelation" has been "the drawing away of the veil of darkness."

Until now you have been in darkness concerning His life, His love, and His power within you.

But God is about to give you a breakthrough into the true knowledge of Him dwelling in your heart.

Believe me, revelation is power!

You will learn to both recognize and break through to His Presence within you. Empowered by His love, you will rise up in a new spirit of victory that will cause all fear to flee.

You say, "Brother Cerullo, what do you mean by a new work of restoration and grace?"

Let me explain.

Throughout the Bible, God has always had two ways of doing things. The first way has been to work from outside His people, bestowing His blessings upon them; in other words, to do things for them.

The second way has been to work in and through them from the inside out.

As an illustration, look at His plan of salvation.

Salvation itself is a two-fold process. First is the work of salvation which Christ accomplished for us through His life, death, and resurrection.

Second is the work that God wants to do within us through His Holy Spirit, empowering us from the inside out.

The first part of salvation is the outward work of God, done for us. The second is His inward work, done within us.

But, for too long, people in the Church have been stuck in a rut, devoid of inner power because they have focused all their attention on what they wanted God to do *for* them ...ignoring the powerful work that He longs to do *in* them.

Thousands of people have come crying to the altar, "Oh, God, I can't get deliverance. Give me the victory over fear."

But God is telling them, "*I put My Son, Jesus, inside you.*"

"*Greater is he that is in you, than he that is in the world.*"

I JOHN 4:4

Stand up on your feet. Call on Him. Fix your faith on Him. Let go of those fears and let Him rise up against them. Let Him expel them from the inside out. When you do, you will never be the same.

For years I've been saying that it's time for the Church to move beyond the point of blessing (what God wants to do for you), into the realm of power (what He wants within you). This is what I've been talking about.

Right now, God wants you to have a breakthrough whereby you stop viewing His grace as simply an outward blessing or favor, and come into the experience of it as the power of Christ within you; the only power that can overcome all fear.

If you have any doubts about God's grace as an actual power or spiritual force within you, listen to what our Lord told the Apostle Paul about the famous "thorn" in his life.

Three times Paul had asked the Lord to remove it (to do all the work for him from the outside). But the Lord told him:

> *"...My grace is sufficient for thee: for my strength is made perfect in weakness."*
>
> II CORINTHIANS 12:9

Believe me, the Lord was not referring to His grace as some type of passive blessing. He was referring to it as a formidable inward force; His assistance within us which, when exercised by Paul, would strengthen him until the apostle—in union with the Lord—could overcome any foe!

This is the very force that God Himself is placing within you now to give you all the breakthrough power you need to completely defeat fear.

> *"For sin shall not (any longer) exert dominion over you, since now you are not under Law (as slaves), but under grace..."*
>
> ROMANS 6.14, AMP

With God's new work of revelation and His new outpouring of grace in your heart, you will now have all the assistance you need in your inner man to be dead to all fears, and alive only to Christ.

You will begin to discover for yourself, *"...it is no longer I who live, but Christ lives in me"* (Galatians 2:20, NKJ).

His astounding love for you will soon begin to break through all the walls you have built out of fear. It will soon penetrate and rule all your thoughts.

This is what it means to be renewed in the spirit of your mind (Ephesians 4:23). All spirits of fear and darkness will be cast out, and the Spirit of God will be in, ruling all you do.

You ask, "When will all this start taking place in my life?"

It will start the moment you agree to stand on your feet and begin saying "no" to the spirit of fear!

That is why this is an important growth period for you. It is a time when you will finally begin to:

"brace up and reinvigorate and set right your slackened and weakened and drooping hands and strengthen your feeble and palsied and tottering knees, And cut through and make firm...straight paths for your feet."

HEBREWS 12:12,13, AMP

This is also a time when our Lord is asking us to, *"be on the watch to look (after one another), to see that no one falls back from and fails to secure God's grace"*(verse 15).

Beloved, once you have begun to stand up and lay hold of God's grace within you, there is one more aspect of your personal relationship with Him that you must understand if you are to maintain total victory over fear.

Chapter 6

THE LOVE THAT CASTS OUT FEAR

From the beginning of time God planned to mightily strengthen you in these last hours.

Before you were even conceived, He knew that He would be giving you a miraculous breakthrough over fear through a new dimension of relationship with His Son.

This is a relationship that is founded and rooted in the power of love...a love so powerful that it has overcome the entire world and every unclean spirit in it!

God tells us, *"There is no fear in love; but perfect love casts out fear, because fear involves torment..."* (I John 4:18, NKJ).

This is a dynamic passage of truth. But before we go any further, let us look at the Amplified Bible's translation of this verse in its entirety. It says:

"There is no fear in love dread does not exist; but full grown [complete, perfect] love turns fear out of doors and expels every trace of terror For fear brings with it the thought of punishment, and [so] be who is afraid has not reached the full maturity of love is not yet grown into love's complete perfection."

I JOHN 4:18 AMP

Take a moment now to reread this passage. Allow it to penetrate deeply into your spirit. For this takes us right into the heart of the reason why some of us fail.

We have read the phrase, "perfect love casts out fear" so many times that we have assumed it is always Jesus' love for us that is to do all the work.

However, there is another way of looking at this.

Remember that we are in a covenant relationship with our Lord and with each other. It is a covenant of love, and love is a two way street.

Therefore, not only is it Christ's powerful love for us that casts out fear; but our love for Him should cause us to stand up in union with Him, and literally kick that spirit of fear right out the door!

Think about it.

When you truly love someone and become one with him, you love what he loves and hate what he hates.

Our relationship with the Lord is no different. Through His Word we are told, *"You who love the LORD, hate evil..."* (Psalm 97:10 NKJ)

There is no worse evil than fear.

This being the case, all of you who truly love Him will fervently desire to no longer tolerate all those fears that are so offensive to Him. You will no longer put up with those vile, fearful thoughts which so brutally block your communion with Him.

From now on, you will rise up and refuse to let any fear pollute your heart and mind.

As soon as you take this stand, something dramatic will begin to happen. You will come into an even deeper revelation of His love for you!

The cry of your heart will change. Instead of it being a constant plea for deliverance, it will be, *"...that I may know Him that I may progressively become more deeply and intimately acquainted with Him..."* (Philippians 3:10, AMP).

And know Him you will. You will come to know Him in a deeper way each time you choose to let your love for Him rise up and, with Him, expel those fears right out of your mind.

He will then rush in to fill all those areas where fear once dwelt, and you are one step closer to being totally restored.

GROW IN LOVE FOR HIM

By now you may be saying, "What can I do? I don't have that kind of love for the Lord yet. I want to...but I'm not quite there." Let me help you. Know that He is right there with you, knocking at the door of your heart, longing to come in (Revelation 3:20). The only problem is that you don't know how to come into the experience of His Presence. You don't know how to "open the door." To help you discover where the block may be, sit down and ask the Holy Spirit to lead you through the following questions:

- Do I really crave and desire His Presence more than anything else in the world, no matter where I am or what the circumstances are?

- Do I take the time each day to meet with Him; to spend time with Him; time when I'm not begging for anything or dictating to Him, but just being still before Him in adoration and worship?

- Do I raise my voice to Him, singing to Him in my heart, praising and thanking Him continually, or do I withhold it because I'm afraid?

- When He asks me to do something, what is my response and how quick is it?

- Am I totally willing to relinquish my fears (which I have become so accustomed to), so that I might dwell quietly in His peace?

- Do I get so caught up in the cares and "works" of this world that I postpone devoting myself to a relationship with Him?

- Does He mean more to me than my reputation, the opinions of others, my family, my possessions, or my ambitions, even my ambitions for Him?

- How much does obedience to Him mean to me? Have I completely given Him my will? What price am I willing to pay?

- Do I have any unpaid vows?

Whatever that price is, please do not be afraid. Make up your mind now that you are willing to pay it.

Chapter 7

WINNING THE WAR VERSUS WINNING THE BATTLE

By now you know how vitally important it is for you to begin today to break through and press on to victory.

In fact, as soon as you read this book you might run right out and win your very first battle against fear.

"Hallelujah!" you'll shout. "It works!"

But don't be deceived. Winning one battle does not mean you've won the war. Until you win your personal battles against fear and any other demon spirits, you're in no shape to get into the real war for other souls.

Wars are made up of many battles. After your first battle is won, you can expect Satan to try to reclaim lost territory by attacking you in three vital areas: your mind, your emotions, and your will.

Remember that Satan is the father of lies. Soon after the victory, he will try to tell you that you were never delivered in the first place. He will try to deceive you by counterfeiting your past symptoms of fear. He will most certainly try to tempt you with the "easy way out" the next time fear comes along.

What do you do?

The Apostle James instructs us, *"Therefore submit to God. Resist the devil and he will flee from you."*

JAMES 4:7, NKJ

Now most of us are pretty good at the submission part, and you can submit all you want. But until you fully determine to also resist Satan, there is no fight; and when there is no fight, he automatically wins.

However, the moment you choose to stand and resist, you establish a turning point in the war. No longer are you merely Satan's pawn to push around; you are someone to contend with.

As soon as you prove to the devil that you mean business, the battle is on.

> "Therefore, put on God's complete armor, that you may be able to resist and stand your ground on the evil day [of danger], and having done all [the crisis demands], to stand [firmly in your place]. Stand therefore bold your ground"
>
> EPHESIANS 6.13,14, AMP

Study the entire sixth chapter of the book of Ephesians for yourself. It holds many keys to spiritual warfare, including the "armor" you must put on for any offensive encounter with the enemy.

(For any time you stand facing him, holding firm, and exposing the spirit of fear by calling him by name, you are on the offensive!)

Of course, you know by now that this kind of warfare is never easy.

Jesus battled so hard in the Garden of Gethsemane that He literally sweat blood. And, if it wasn't easy for Jesus, it won't be easy for you.

The price of not fighting is perpetual immaturity and spiritual stagnation. The writer of Hebrews warned of this when he admonished believers who were falling behind:

> "You have not yet struggled and fought agonizingly against sin, nor have you resisted and withstood to the point of pouring out your [own] blood."
>
> HEBREWS 12:4, AMP

After 37 years of victorious spiritual warfare, I can tell you that it is at the point when you literally feel (in the spirit) that your own blood is about to be poured out, that God's power sweeps into your being like a flood, and the enemy is gone! Is spiritual warfare pretty? No. Will your war against fear be pretty? No. Do you want to grow and be useful to God? Yes! Since you do, God has equipped you with all you need to do it.

> *"For the weapons of our warfare are not carnal, but mighty in God for pulling down strongholds, casting down imaginations, and every high thing that exalteth itself against the knowledge of God, and bringing into captivity every thought to the obedience of Christ."*
>
> II CORINTHIANS 10:4,5

Again, casting down every wayward imagination and bringing every fearful thought to the obedience of Christ will be agonizing at first ...but you are not alone. It is all a part of qualifying for God's Army! The Apostle Peter described a blow by blow account of these spiritual battles (and their outcomes) when he said:

> *"...that enemy of yours, the devil, roams around like a lion roaring [in fierce hunger], seeking someone to seize upon and devour...Withstand him; be firm in faith [against his onset]—rooted, established, strong, immovable and determined] knowing that the same [identical] sufferings are appointed to your brotherhood...throughout the world. And after you have suffered a little while, the God of all grace...will Himself complete and make you what you ought to be, establish and ground you securely, and strengthen and settle you. To Him be the dominion [power, authority, rule] forever and ever. Amen [so be it].*
>
> I PETER 5:8-11, AMP

GET READY FOR SPLIT SECOND DECISIONS

The United States has an advance military warning system which warns us if missiles have been fired from Russia. If they have, we have only ten minutes to wage a counter offensive attack against the enemy.

Well, I've got news for you. When that demon spirit of fear launches one of his "fear missiles" at your mind, you don't have ten minutes to wait. You have one split second in which to decide to counterattack.

This decision takes advance preparation. You must be prepared to instantly choose for the Lord and not against Him.

What do I mean?

I mean that it is possible to have all the knowledge of what to do, all the grace of God to do it, all the forces of heaven standing by to help you overcome fear, and still, in that last split second when the enemy roars, decide to deny God's power and once again go down to defeat.

The choice is yours.

What can you do to get ready to choose Christ in an instant?

Have your sword ready!

"Let the high praises of God be in their throat and a two edged sword in their hand"

Psalm 149:6, AMP

Have scriptures that banish fear, and praises of your Lord ready in your heart and on your tongue. Your sword of the Spirit is the Word of God, fueled by your love for Him.

When the enemy looms on the horizon, use your weapons!

Speak them. Bind the enemy and defeat him with the

Word. Let Christ arise within you. Let His enemies be scattered! You are the victorious one!

Decide right now to put on a new mental attitude toward the battles ahead. Put on a spirit of fierce determination, and make up your mind that you will choose to press through every time.

The Apostle Paul expressed this same valiant determination when he said:

> *"Not that I have already attained, or am already perfected; but I press on, that I may lay hold of that for which Christ Jesus has also laid hold of me. Brethren, I do not count myself to have apprehended; but one thing I do, forgetting those things which are behind and reaching forward to those things which are ahead, I press toward the goal for the prize of the upward call of God in Christ Jesus."*
> PHILIPPIANS 3:12-14, NKJ

Then Paul went on to say, *"Therefore, let us, as many as are mature; have this mind; and if in anything you think otherwise, God will reveal even this to you"* (verse 15).

Beloved, one day each one of us, like the servants in the book of Matthew, will stand before our Master and account for every talent He has given us.

But also appearing before the throne of God will be countless souls of our generation crying out to the Father, *"The harvest is past, the summer is ended, and we are not saved"* (Jeremiah 8:20).

Each year over 120 million people are added to the world's population—unreached and unsaved.

How can any one of us, knowing what and Whom we have been given, stand by and let any demon spirit of fear hold us back while millions face eternal death?

The summer is almost over. The end-time harvest is nearly finished. Countless souls still have not heard, and we will be accountable for each one of them.

Can you hear God's battle cry in your heart?

He is calling to you now, saying:

"Have not I commanded you? Be strong vigorous and very courageous; be not afraid, neither be dismayed; for the Lord your God is with you wherever you go."

JOSHUA 1:9, AMP

Wherever you go, break through and press on in the mighty name of Jesus!

You are free from fear.

There is a greater anointing upon me now than ever before to pray for your needs.

Never before, in my more than 55 years of frontline ministry have I carried a deeper burden for the Body of Christ than I do now.

I have prayed, fasted, interceded, agonized and fought spiritual warfare against satanic powers...

and God gave me a vision!

God said..."Place the needs of my people upon the altar before My Presence...Jesus is praying for all their needs to be met!"

A vision of Jesus Christ, our Great High Priest, praying for all your needs.

God said, "Place the needs of my people upon the altar before My Presence. Jesus is praying for all their needs to be met."

Every need, every disease, every family problem, every circumstance...God wants me to lift your need for Jesus to pray for you. Do not delay. Write all your needs on the following page and mail it to me today!

Brother Cerullo,

Please place these requests on the Miracle Prayer Altar and pray for these needs:

_____

_____

_____

_____

_____

_____

❏ Enclosed is my love gift of $(£)_____ to help you win souls and to support this worldwide ministry.

❏ Please tell me how I can become a God's Victorious Army member...to help you reach the nations of the world, and receive even more anointed teaching on a monthly basis!

Name _____

Address _____

City _____ State or Province _____

Postal Code _____ Phone Number (____)_____

E-mail_____

Mail today to:

MORRIS CERULLO WORLD EVANGELISM

San Diego: P.O. Box 85277 • San Diego, CA 92186

Canada: P.O. Box 3600 • Concord, Ontario L4K 1B6

U.H.: P.O. Box 277 • Hemel Hempstead, Herts HP2 7DH